MANNERS FOR MILLIONAIRES

MANNERS FOR MILLIONAIRES

Brummell & Beau

THE BRITISH LIBRARY

First published in 1900 by Simpkin, Marshall & Co.

This edition published in 2014 by
The British Library
96 Euston Road
London NW1 2DB

British Library Cataloguing in Publication Data
A catalogue record for this publication is available from The British Library

ISBN 978 0 7123 5724 1

© The British Library 2014

Printed in Hong Kong by Great Wall Printing Co. Ltd

CONTENTS.

PREFATORY NOTE.

THE coloured plates specially prepared for this volume had at the last moment to be omitted owing to the unfortunate indisposition of the Academician employed, but rather than disappoint the Public we have inserted instead a few specimen woodcuts from a forthcoming treatise on British Fishes. We trust that, in a work intended primarily to instruct, these beautiful and interesting creatures may not be considered entirely out of place. The author of the treatise in question asks us to state that they are published in this book under protest.

MANNERS FOR MILLIONAIRES

CHAPTER I.

'IN THE PADDOCK.'

(*An Introduction.*)

SINCE that epoch when, at the urgent instigation of many of our peers, we were induced to publish certain explicit directions concerning the Deportment of Dukes, we have not ceased to receive constant communications not only from those in the most exalted circles, whose lives have been ennobled, and whose actions have been chastened thereby, but also from numberless Respectables unknown to the *Almanach de Gotha.*

From one section in particular the cry for instruction and guidance has been loud and prolonged, and with no uncertain voice the Plutocracy of Great Britain, her Colonies, and the two Americas, call upon us to come down and help them.

'What we needs,' says a distinguished Australian Mutton King, ' is Varnish. My 'eart's in the right place, but set me down afore a bowl of peas, and which 'and 'olds the knife is more'n I can tell you.'

Another appeal comes from a young lady who, she informs us, resides near the Zoological Gardens, and always goes into mourning with the Court.

'Should Papa wear whiskers? I only saw three sets in the Park last Sunday, and one was pro-Boer!'

A third correspondent asks us, ' Should I take a Grouse-moor for Whitsuntide, or is a Stud-farm smarter?'

By a fourth we are requested to—' Send a good anecdote, by return, to tell to a nobleman, something about me and a horse, if possible.'

A fifth inquires, ' How can I become known as a *Gourmand* (pronounced *chef* and meaning *impresario*)? When Port has gone tawny does it need to be shaken, and how can Claret be corked, also, is everything that's yellow Sherry, and how does one begin an Asparagus?'

Yet another writes: 'The Marchesa Sparghetti del Fuego Macchiavelli has called by mistake. Can I say she dropped a parcel and return her visit? It is our best chance so far.'

But besides these gratifying testimonials to our discrimination, we receive another stream of correspondence. This comes, though it will scarcely be credited, from such as actually desire to incur the responsibilities of wealth.

'I want a steam yacht, a new collapsible Opera-hat, and a shooting-box with a good salmon stream within five minutes' walk; and I am tired of wintering in Shaftesbury Avenue,' writes one. 'At present I am paid 1*l*. 16*s*. 9*d*. a-week. This must be increased. I enclose stamps, and am,

'Yours respectfully, Soho.'

Another pathetic letter begins: 'Things have not prospered recently. I used to compose the Menus in "Diners and Dynasties" for the *Charing Cross Gazette*. In fact, I am the original "Lord Mucus Membrayne." But the jealousy of a captious rival disclosed the fact that *Bête blanc* no longer meant whitebait, and I find myself at liberty to push my fortunes otherwise.'

And it ends with these striking words, 'With encouragement, capital, luck, and a good wife, I believe I should be capable of better things.'

It will thus be seen that we cater for no narrow coterie, for no exclusive class of the community. Our menu (to borrow an image from our amiable correspondent's letter) includes dishes adjusted to any appetite; our wine list, vintages attuned to the most comprehensive thirst.

CHAPTER II.

'FLUSHING THE COVEY.'

(A Sparkling Start.)

FROM the preceding chapter it will be clear that such of our readers as still belong to the Pauper, Practically Pauper, and Comparatively Pauper strata of society—those, we mean, with less than 5000*l.* a year and fewer than seventeen spare bedrooms—will naturally feel grateful for a few introductory directions towards ameliorating their condition.

Inasmuch as the most palatial edifices rear their proud pinnacles on a regimen of strawless brick, and the Giants of Intellect and Industry spring toothless from undecorated protoplasm to eventually crack and masticate the nut of destiny, so the plush-clad Dives of to-morrow must start untrammelled as the fustianed Lazarus of to-day.

Similarly it is proverbial that 'No Means is no end of a Justification,' or, as the French say, if you wish to be *riche* you must start *de nouveau*. Therefore lend your motor-car to the milkman, dismiss your valet, distribute your wardrobe, warehouse your family, and raffle your pyjamas.*

With a single sixpence (or dollar) in your pocket, proceed on foot to an industrial Centre (or Center) and apply for thirteen or fourteen unsuitable situations. This will inure you to bear disappointments upon your return to Society.

In order that your success may be justly attributed to your Principles rather than to your Principal, it is also as well at this period to learn by rote a few such admirable maxims as :—

'It is always too early to lend.'

'Steel thyself, trust not without, that men may not Steel Trust without thee,' &c. &c.

We have actually known an elderly 'Gent' (his own *nom*

* These, together with your appetite and conscience, may of course be recovered when your modest ambitions are fulfilled.

de genre) forced by the importunity of a halfpenny periodical to invent his youthful rules of conduct in the seclusion of his alabaster bath.

The precise channel into which your energies should now be turned is a matter of comparatively small moment. All roads lead to Rome—for one who can decipher the finger-posts. Besides, your Roman grandson will have to forget how you came there. Among lucrative avocations we may, however, in passing mention the following :—

Finding an escape of oil under the bath-room floor ; discovering that the sparkling object your friends mistook for a broken soap-dish is really the projecting lode of a diamond reef; constructing nutritious beverages out of hitherto neglected quadrupeds; and realising the fact that people will swallow anything if they are thirsty enough (although it must always be remembered that 'two swallows do not make a brewery pay ').

By the strict observance of these simple directions you will soon find yourself placed beyond the reach of immediate want No doubt, for some time to come, your sleeve-links will still have to be of undressed gun-metal, and your hunger appeased by a modest meal of spring chicken and marmalade pudding, but you can begin sitting for your portrait, and unclaimed lots in Park Lane should be noted.

CHAPTER III

'THE PUSH STROKE.'

(*Dives Demonstrative.*)

ALTHOUGH the rules in the previous chapter have hitherto supplied their fortunate countries with a tolerably large Plutocracy, we cannot help thinking that one method of increasing this beneficent class has been most unaccountably overlooked. Would it not be possible to call attention in some unobtrusive way, that one need not be ashamed of afterwards, to gifts that might otherwise suffer through neglect, and virtues that might wither for lack of a little kindly encouragement? Everything, even the haughty house of Harmsworth, must have a beginning; and to our embryo Midas we would say, ' Begin to push yourself a little.' Supposing, for instance, that we ourselves should feel convinced, notwithstanding our embarrassing diffidence, that we had some really meritorious article to introduce to the public, which, if disposed of in sufficient quantity, would enable us to resign the practice of letters for the enjoyments of Ermined Ease and Gilded Licence, we should proceed somewhat after this fashion. In a quiet and unostentatious but nevertheless confident manner we should inform the public of the benefit to themselves to be procured by the use of the aforesaid article. A brief legend to this effect, displayed where the literate wayfarer might see it, would answer the purpose admirably. It might, for example, be traced in simple lettering on a series of second-hand locomotives, which might then be urged slowly through the traffic of, let us say, the Strand, while the blowing of a steam syren might call the attention of the careless.

Or this idea, which struck us lately when sauntering beneath the opulent foliage of our deer park, could, we are sure, be advantageously employed for the same purpose. Nature in her more agreeable aspects is, no doubt, pleasing to the refined eye and soothing to the cultured understanding. But, if nature unadorned has this satisfactory effect, what limits are there to the enjoyable sensations which might be obtained were her elegance embellished by the ingenuity of man?

Supposing one were to weave the legend mentioned above into the sylvan or aquatic harmonies of Spring. For example, instead of looking upon an unbroken and therefore somewhat monotonous line of trees or mountains, supposing they were to

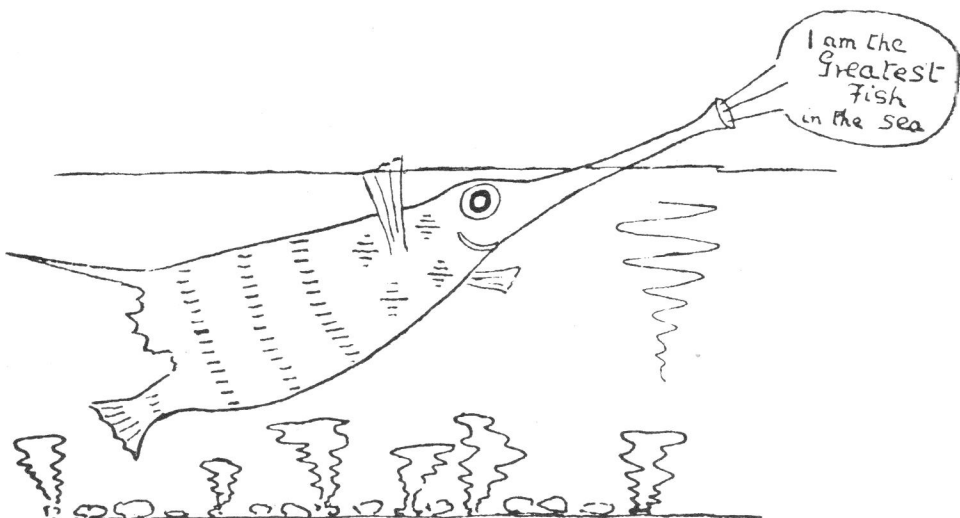

THE STARICUS STRIPICUS, OR BLOW-YOUR-OWN-TRUMPET FISH.

be partially concealed behind a neat deal hoarding, designed roughly to represent the back of a stately warehouse, with the message you wished to convey inscribed prettily in gamboge upon a ground of ultramarine, would it not be admirably calculated to arouse the intelligent interest of the least thoughtful?

Of course, it should ever be borne in mind that the attention of the self-absorbed Public is with great difficulty arrested, and with greater difficulty retained, and so the genuine Altruist, conscious of the far-reaching benefits which his inspiration would confer upon the Many, will on no account be deterred from his ultimate object by the fact that some temporary inconvenience may be, incidentally, occasioned to the Few.

The following ingenious scheme was proposed by us to a retiring young Scientist, who had invented an infallible but little-known preparation acting in a soothing and beneficent manner upon the scalp, the tubercles of the lung, and especially the nervous system; and it was lately put into execution with the very happiest results.

At a pre-arranged signal, sixteen gasometers were simultaneously exploded in a crowded district of his native town.

The effect was said to be most striking, and the resulting fire raged for upwards of a fortnight, while the loss of nerve-tone sustained by the inhabitants flattered our predictions, and the demand for the preparation in question (which was ejected in packets by the force of the concussion, and fell as it were like manna) exceeded even the most sanguine expectations.

Pursuing still further the same line of thought, the daring notion strikes us that this method of winning the Laurels of Assiduity and the Bays of Merit might be adapted to a more personal use. As the world at present wags, the bashfulness of the Millionaire, and the assurance of the younger son, give rise to the most embarrassing misunderstandings. Lest a hypersensitive society should have to reproach itself with neglected opportunities, would it not be a convenient and a cheerful thing if Ability paraded Piccadilly with a gong, and Ambition cantered to the Carlton on a camel? Nothing, we may remind our readers, looks worse than a too ostentatious modesty. We have known a diffident Prelate suspected of arson through not writing his own name on his cheques.

Could we ourselves be induced to bound over the paling of anonymity into the glare of empurpled notoriety, we should be inclined to begin with a scandal. This need not be a serious affair, but if the Primate could be discovered beneath our sideboard with the missing ace half swallowed, if we could induce our Consorts to become addicted to a Jeunesse Dorée (Vital Spark), or if our opiumed yearling should unexpectedly stop at Tattenham Corner, interest we believe might be stirred.

After this, we should purchase, and, to the best of our ability, edit a jaundiced journal; contracting at the same time a bigamous alliance.

Next we should don trunk hose in the Green Park, and publish our correspondence with General De Wet; and as a final resort we think we should feel tempted to let our hair grow and dabble in literature of the Eternal City and Suburban type.

If our privacy were still respected at the end of this course, we should give it up, feeling that we were doomed to be mere gentlemen.

CHAPTER IV

'*'CROSS COUNTRY.'*

(*Crœsus in Chrysalis.*)

ASSUMING that our readers are now ascending the stair-case of Prosperity, aided by the handrail of this treatise, they will no doubt feel some excusable trepidation as the first landing is attained, or, dropping this simile (which has been selected out of many others), they are now worth 5000*l.* a-year, and their laudable ambition is naturally to behave as they conceive they should in the situation to which Providence has manifestly beckoned them.

' Am I justified in exchanging Pedronella for a larger poodle, and what should you advise about keeping a landau-lette ?   It is seven minutes to the station, and Pedronella's hair is beginning to come out.'   One gentleman (or, if we may judge from the handwriting, his wife) writes to us in these words.

'Certainly,' we reply, 'purchase, or, better still, hire the landaulette; but would not a thorough top-dressing of Petroleum, applied with a camel-hair brush, preserve Pedronella for a few years longer? It is not well to make too violent a transition in the present state of securities.'

Another writer addressed us thus :—

'Would *Multum in Parvo* do for a motto, and what does it mean? My wife wants a design for the new serviette rings, and the crest is to be taken from something we saw in the Crystal Palace. Also, would it be quite nobby to grow the same in snowdrops on the drying green?'

We responded as follows:—

'The last interrogation we should answer heartily in the affirmative, but would not *Quid pro quo* be safer for the motto? The quotation you propose would have to be applied with considerable discrimination, and unless the translation is thoroughly mastered we should prefer our own suggestion. Before finally deciding on the crest, would it not be well to also search the Westminster Aquarium?'

16

These two letters, with their replies, which we have intentionally given *in extenso* (another excellent motto, by the way), cover most of the pitfalls at this stage.

Let us now assume that five figures have been reached, first-class travelling has become a necessity, and the eldest son is preparing for Eton. By this time Pedronella's faithful tail wags in a fairer world, what is left of the landaulette has been given to the Vicar, and there are rumours of mail-clad Ancestors, whose slogan of *Multum in Parvo!* retrieved the day at Crecy.

These last should, if possible, be now arranged in the order in which they may be confidently assumed to have been born, the locality of the ancient family estates ascertained, and the whole brought up to date with the assistance of the Heralds' College, and published in a neat half-calf binding. A good title might be something like this—

'THE PLUTOS OF MONK'S PLUTTON,
DOLLAR ABBEY and SHAIRTON HOLDER.
With some observations on other families of the name.
By BLANC GRIPHON, Knight Unicorn-at-arms, F.S.A.
Dedicated to JAMES ROBERT PLUTO, ESQ., of Sydenham'

This work will, perhaps, be displayed to the best advantage if laid upon a simple Moorish pedestal beside an Etruscan vase containing daffodils.

Much instruction may be gained by studying the following, and our answer to it :—

'I hear that a Baronet of my name, only spelled with y's, was killed by an arrow at Waterloo. Were Baronets always married and had issues, my wife says so, and if so am I the heir ? Also, is Southend fashionable this season, and can the Guards' Club be recommended ? Is it up to my class ?'

To this we reply :—

'Unquestionably you are as much the deceased Baronet's heir as can reasonably be expected. The spelling is quite near enough for genealogical purposes. We should, however, advise you to alter either the arrow or the battlefield. Why not make it Hastings ? Such an incident did, we believe, occur there. Southend we ourselves scarcely consider to be as exclusive as some other places ; but possibly we are prejudiced. The Guards' Club is perfectly respectable, but we foresee obstacles. Why not try the Junior Constitutional ?'

And now we will suppose that by sterling industry and undeviating rectitude our readers have left far down below, and scarcely recognisable, their effeter companions of the Mart and Mill, and have attained at length that perfumed

VULGARIS TOPHUS, OR SUN AND AIR FISH.

alcove at the summit of the staircase where the golden pavement, burnished by the footprints of the Opulent, reflects the effulgence of their fame. (This means that he has become a millionaire).

19

It is by such that we are most frequently consulted on the nicest questions of conscience and refinement.

' Is Tottie vulgar ? ' writes one ; ' and should it be changed to Gwendoline ? Also can I allow her to marry the Nephew of a Cardinal? Nobody can ever tell he is anybody in particular unless you explain.'

Our reply lies before us as we write : —

' My dear Sir, — A man of your income can call his daughter anything he likes, but we cannot bring ourselves to approve of the Nephew. Have you tried the Uncle ?

' Yours, &c.'

Finally, before quitting this portion of our subject, we shall give a few simple general rules of conduct, and, that they may be more easily assimilated and rise to the mind more readily in an emergency, we have, at considerable trouble, thrown them into the poetic form :—

Cultivate those who don't want to know you,
But cut such as need you whatever you do.

We have known many an alderman ascribe his respectability to this precept alone.

Those who propose to rush heedlessly into Philanthropy as a profession would do well to take warning from this pregnant couplet :—

> Never retain an old friend who's no use,
> Finding a job for his children's the Deuce.

Such as have a female child should note the advice contained in the following :—

> A Bart. in the hand's worth a Peer on the bough ;
> She'll never be younger, there's no time like now.

We will conclude this chapter by calling attention to the following fine piece of prose :—

Here we leave our Millionaire, towering solitary, cloud-capped and Jovian, straddling Colossus-like across the turbid stream of less shrewd opportunists, and heedless alike of the glow-worm of unprofitable Fancy and the gargoyle of unpractical Romance.

CHAPTER V.

'THE HOME HOLE.'

(*Crœsus in Clover.*)

WE have now indicated the way and staked the course from Penury to Plenty—from Anxiety to Affluence.

The Really Rich are at last, under our guidance, securely placed on their pedestals of Gold. The sapphire shrine no longer awaits the gorgeous god.

Inasmuch as the crystal Casket must be fitly fashioned for the Gold Fish, so must the Mansion be moulded to the Millionaire.

The initial difficulty is the selection of an eligible site. This has increased, curiously enough, *pari passu* with the enlargement of the population. We would, therefore, urge the

22

Plutocrat who recognises the necessity of securing a suitable demesne, to study carefully the following general principles before placing his cheque-book in the hands of his Architects.

Central and commanding sites for building purposes in the Metropolis are of course plentiful and easily acquired, but many of them present to the Observant certain objections.

For instance, the Horse Guards' Parade is still used for the trooping of the Colours and the distribution of War Medals.

Trafalgar Square is handy for the Theatres, but the National Liberal Club is somewhat too close, and, now we come to think of it, the site is overlooked by an unfashionable Picture Gallery.

The British Museum (if the name were changed to 'de Beer' Buildings or Tammany Towers) could, after slight alteration, be recommended as a comfortable town Villa for the Season, but the stabling is indifferent, and we understand there is no Toilet Saloon nearer than Southampton Row.

All things being considered we would rather suggest that an extra-mural site be selected, where the temperate pleasures of the country could be brought into touch with the exotic gaiety of the City by means of a simple electric mono-railway. First, then, decide upon the particular County you intend to honour (or honor); next dig a deep hole, place the mansion firmly upon the contents, and stock the cavity with pike and salmon.

Fringe the spiral drive with Cedars from Lebanon or Giants from the Yosemite Valley according as your hereditary instinct dictates, and see that the Picture Gallery is more than sufficiently extensive to accommodate the Ancestral Portraits you have ordered. (Possible Posterity must not be forgotten.)

The Humming-bird—and Zebra—kennels should be built largely of glass, and will probably attract more attention if securely lashed to the summit of the Water Tower.

The chief entrance to the edifice should occupy approximately the centre of the main façade, and should coincide as far as practicable with the termination of the drive. The opening should be of such calibre (or caliber) that egress may be accomplished with rapidity and comfort. Its exact situation may be pleasantly indicated by the mat on one side and the sentry-box on the other.

Only the finest Tasmanian tin should be employed in the

construction of the Heronry, and the Golf Course should be laid down at right angles to this.

The Curfew (dimly seen through the bath-room window) ought not to be apparent till nearly sundown, and it should then be done by some of the butlers as slowly as possible.

The cistern should be composed of non-inflammable material, and a tumbler placed beside it.

The other appointments of the Château should be strictly in keeping with whatever traditions its illustrious owner intends to borrow or adopt.

The Establishment—which term does not necessarily include the Tenantry, but may be allowed to embrace the Governess—should comprise at least one Chaplain.

While the Completed Capitalist will appreciate the advisability of keeping a paternal eye upon the selection of the Lady-Housemaids and the Scullion-Wenches, he may safely entrust the provision of the remaining members of the Ménage to the Senior Housekeeper.

Explicit instructions should, however, be given that all Foresters, Deer-stalkers, Mole-catchers, and Under-beaters be distinguished from the other henchmen by a difference in the colour of the cockade.

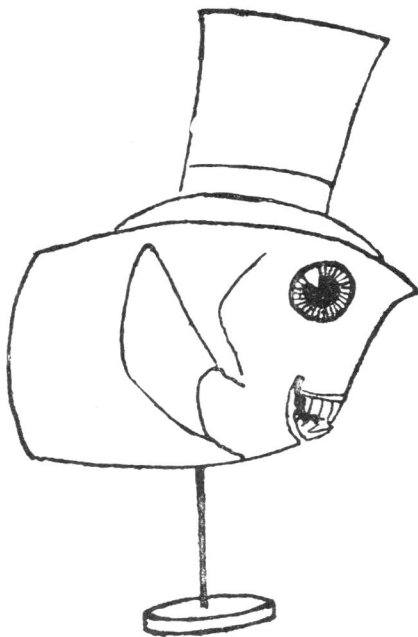

HEAD OF SYNDICATUS INNOCENS, OR TRUST SHARK.

We are unable to commend the modern ostentation of maintaining a separate private Executioner, however characteristic he might be as a hereditary relic. But, on the other hand, nothing is more likely to lubricate the luxuries of the pampered Oligarch, to sooth the turmoil of a tender conscience, to pave the way to permanent placidity, and to drown the inanities of post-prandial conversation than the perpetual presence of a Pensioned Minstrel. He may be a stalwart MacOssian with his Pibroch (in which case the capercailzie should be roasted whole), or a seductive Sadducee with his Jew's Harp, or per-chance a Choctaw with his American Organ, but, happier inspiration than all, a plutocratic acquaintance has even accli-matised the romantic Troubadour of Provence.

This finished bard has already supplied his patron with the following delicate effusions:

The first is dedicated to his friend and master:—

'Now, what about the Manners of the Millionairy Man?
   He never knows he shouldn't, and he always thinks
      he can.
   The things he can't remember are the very things he
      ought,
   And he knows some quaint Commandments that
      Moses never taught.'

27

The next appears to be a tribute to the virtues of the Chatelaine:—

'And what about my Methods with the Millionairy M'am?
Well, I haven't yet explained to her exactly who I am.
But I make a casual reference to my friendship with "His Grace,"
And I let it be imagined that I have a Country Place.'

Now follows a fragment of even tenderer sentiment:—

'But what about the Merits of the Millionairy Miss?
She's rich enough to marry, and she's sweet enough to kiss.
In truth she's so bewitching, that I often wish that I
Had a prospect of succeeding to a peerage by-and-by.'

The last was obviously stimulated by the enthusiasm associated with the Coming-of-age festivities of the youthful Scion :—

'Oh, what about the Morals of the Millionairy Mug?
He's a weakness for the ladies and a fondness for the jug,

And when his Millionairy Dad bequeaths him the
    Estate,
Some Millionairy ducks and drakes he's sure to in-
    cubate.'

Thus lapped in the purple of his sybarite nest, protected by obsequious solicitude and perennial homage, and lulled by the incense of sycophantic roundelays, our readers can hardly fail to bestow upon their *vade mecum* and its conscientious authors a passing spasm of gratitude.

We ask no testimonial, however: the prosperity we have procured for our *protégés* is the only earthly reward we seek.

CHAPTER VI.

'LE JEU EST FAIT.'

(*Midas Amused.*)

FROM that remoter age when man first hounded the ichthyosaurus with the poisoned boulder and volleyed the bounding discobolus against the dedans of some preadamite precipice, up to this era of the Croquet Expert and the lithe Ping-pongster, the constant cry of the Organism has been 'Mens conscia in corpore vile' (meaning 'Better a century for Derby than a cycle through Cathay'). Fortunate is he who, untramelled by the necessity for toil, can devote his riper adolescence to the cult of Jehu and guard the wicket of Hygiene with the bunker of Affluence!

It is no light matter to apportion the Millionaire to his exercise. A personage of considerable Transatlantic reputation, the fortunate possessor of eighteen railroads, a ducal son-in-law, and a chronic dyspepsia, remarked to us the other day that it was not always easy to discover a diversion which should be consistent with his Income without overtaxing his Capacity.

'I used to play Hop Scotch when I didn't have to be so particular about style,' he complained; 'I once won three dollars at Pitch and Toss out West, and there was a game with marbles I played bully ; but a man worth twenty millions of your money can't play them things now. Horses never was in my platform, Golf is too tarnation profane for a man with sins enough already to think of, and Bridge ain't the kind of exercise I need. What's a man to do?'

We sent him to fish in the Serpentine while we thought the matter over, and we now have much pleasure in presenting our friend and his fellow-oligarchs with the following results of our reflections.

In the first place it is necessary to distinguish between the Aristoplute and the Plebioplute. By the Aristoplute we mean such as hug the high ambition of owning a Derby winner; by the Plebioplute him who publicly shakes hands with the

31

friends of his youth, observing that he envies them their innocent integrity.

When the former takes his managing clerk into partnership with a view to devoting himself to his tenantry and statecraft, he will become conscious of a growing desire to excel in those manly and invigorating pursuits characteristic of a Feudal Superior. To the Aristoplute, therefore, we should strongly recommend our striking novelty, the Animated Guinea Fowl. This sportsmanlike animal (which can be made to cost as much as a guinea a feather, hence the name) is hatched from an egg after the customary preliminaries and in the usual way. From its birth upwards it supplies a convincing reason for the presence on the estate of a body of Retainers numerous enough to satisfy the most exacting Self-respect. These may be arrayed in any livery the Lord of the Manor desires, but we might suggest that khaki or tartan with sun-helmets, puttees, and imitation Victoria Crosses on the breast, make a pleasing harmony with the antique walls of the family mansion and the placid waters of the teeming fish-pond.

The bird is then taught to leave the bag or coop and approach its patron whenever it hears the dinner-call, which it has been taught to associate with the discharge of his fowling-piece. This should ensure capital sport upon the opening day of the season (of which the press should be supplied with particulars).

Although this ingenious contrivance will go far towards the filling the chinks in a well-ordered Patrician life, yet as the French philosopher wittily observed, '*Le sport est bon, mais plus sport est plus bon.*'

We should therefore next recommend our Hygienic Tally-ho Gee - gee to the notice of the Aristoplute, and more particularly of his son and heir. It is an incontestible fact that while the family tree is still in process of cultivation, and the De Butters of Butter-milk Manor are being satisfactorily dissociated from Butter's Blameless Margarine, nothing will more readily divert attention from this operation than the spectacle of the Scion astride our invaluable quadruped. Mounted upon the sleek, curveting creature, pursuing the carted stag betwixt the hedgerows of some shady lane with the execrations peculiar to the Nimrods of the Shires, he will make indeed a dazzling contrast to his inferiors in station. We have even known a doting father (not yet De Buttered) so

PROSPERUS BRITANNICUS, OR JOHN TORY.

34

intoxicated with this proud panorama as to register it as a trade mark.

The Plebioplute will naturally seek somewhat different diversions. Having a genuine admiration for the simple and unpolished virtues which have driven the Wolf from his door to return only with a subscription list, and adorned the horny hands of Toil with the gaiters of Substance, he will wish to amuse himself as he conceives a Plain Man should. As, however, his plain friends, if he consults them, will probably rise to the occasion by recommending him to purchase an ironclad and convert it into a summer-house, or hire a pyramid and furnish it as an aviary, we beg to bring our own novelties in this line under his notice.

What he desires is of course simply air and exercise in a form which not even his unsuccessful brothers-in-law can term frivolous or unproductive. Let him then try our Cane-handled Rebounding Pick-axe. This is a delightful instrument, as vividly recalling the old days of happy toil and innocent festivity as a Californian expletive or a whiff of rye whisky. It practically works itself, and in five hours will convert a stone drinking fountain into an ornamental rockery. Nothing can be calculated to add more to the amenities of his unpretentious cottage, whether by the sands of Newport or among the picturesque fastnesses of the Scottish Highlands.

Should this prove a success, we should be further encouraged to recommend our new Automatic Turning Lathe. This will turn in any direction and upon the slightest provocation. By merely keeping the foot upon the soft pedal, while the mind is at liberty to meditate upon the fluctuations of the market, any number of appropriate and beautiful articles are discharged through a slit in the base. A model of a furniture van containing all the requisites for a real racing stable, an imitation tea-caddy embossed with shamrocks, a group showing Mr. Rockefeller striking oil, and a coronetted tap discharging arsenicated fluid are among the favourites. When exhausted, the apparatus can easily be refilled by the makers.

Thus equipped, neither section of our readers should have any difficulty in whiling away a wet Sunday or a leisured decade. Other resources are no doubt obtainable, but we think the selection we have given should, as Voltaire remarks :—

'Savoir faire

Dans cette galère.'

CHAPTER VII.

'THE CHECK.'

(*Munificent Midas.*)

WHAT shall I do with my millions? No question is more frequently put to us. How to get rid of these incumbrances appears to be for one portion of society as pressing a question as to how to embarrass oneself with them is for the other.

'I can't 'alf enjoy my breakfast for thinking of 'em,' remarked a recently created Viscount of the Holy Roman Empire. 'Luxury and fizz and that, is all very well, but a man don't get what I call really spoke about till he stumps up 'andsome—if it's only for a Scotch University.'

In an equally laudable spirit a retired Chicago operator said to us recently:—

'You just find me two thousand deserving widders and

kids, and I'll fill 'em that full of my best canned goods they can't do no more'n roll down hill. Trust me for seeing it gets into the papers—every dollar of it, Sir!'

It is, then, evident that more is necessary than merely getting rid of the ballast. It must go overboard with a splash.

The following scheme, we think, would be an almost ideal arrangement. By the simple expedient of multiplying the figures by 5 they may be converted into dollars.

	£	s.	d.
To supplying grateful birthplace with Fire-engine (helmets, hose, and horses complete) ; bandstand outside railway-station ; and statues of monarch and Liptifeller in High Street and Market Square . . . . say	250,000	0	0

(Real fire-engine and life-size statues are covered by this sum.)

To endowment of Liptifeller College, establishment of Liptifeller Reference Library

in connection therewith, and branch-line
to Liptifeller Station . . . . say £5,000,000 17 6

(An excellent education, including
the use of the bar-bells can be obtained
for this donation.)

To erection of Liptifeller Mausoleum and
Monument in grounds of Liptifeller
College; figures of Faith, Modesty,
and Enterprise, 14 ft. × 10 ft.;
Recumbent Liptifeller, in marble,
24 ft. × 16 ft. 750,000 10 0

To annual Liptifeller Supper at St. James's
Restaurant for those of name of Liptifeller, and other deserving persons, together with one lady each. Evening
dress indispensable, and toast of ' Liptifeller Aloft ! ' drunk immediately after that
of the Archbishop of Canterbury, say . . 100,000 2 0

(The odd shillings should be de-
voted entirely to the attendants.)

To electoral campaigns and upkeep of fortunate constituency, including sub-scriptions for new Steeple, Cricket Club, trapeze in dancing academy, and mac-adamised approach to swimming-bath,

say £1,000,000 0 0

(This may sound excessive, but Patriotism is expensive.)

Or, as a simple alternative to the above :—

To assisting Liberal Party to maintain requisite relays of Leaders, or Conser-vative Party to propagate Peace and Pom-poms, including (in either case) creation of Baron Liptifeller . . . .

(Same sum and same comment.)

To sundries, such as smaller statues in less important boroughs, conciliating Hibernia, and other unostentatious deeds of kindness —— any sum you do not think you will miss.

CHAPTER VIII.

'THE AMERICA CUP.'

(*Columbia Cocktailed.*)

NOTHING can more eloquently illustrate the wide-spread interest taken in our efforts to alleviate the burden of wealth than the fact that three fire-proof safes (two large and one small) are already filled with our Transatlantic correspondence alone.

We regret that we are not personally acquainted with the Western Hemisphere, and, though we have met several of its inhabitants upon the Rhine, and have studied with some care the voyages of Columbus and the speeches of Mr. Bryan, with a special view to this chapter, yet we confess to finding the inquiries of our Blood-is-thicker-than-water-Kinsmen-over-the-seas sometimes rather difficult to answer satisfactorily.

41

What are we to say, for instance, to the liberty-loving descendant of Pocahontas and the Pilgrim Fathers who writes to us from No. 4076, 359th St., Benjaminfranklinville, in the following terms?—

'I have just read a book about knights in armour and splintering a lance. We have better men in this little place than all the Paladins who ever staggered out of a bar sinister— Hobson before he was kissed and Dewey before he was married, for instance. At the same time, I should be obliged if you would inform me where I can obtain a moated keep, not younger than William Rufus, standing on an inaccessible precipice emblazoned with a few gules' nests, with rights of pit and gallows attached if possible, and a genuine breach made by an arquebus.

'I can go to 176,000 dollars, but for this sum should expect a working portcullis.

'It must be situated in a good hunting country within easy reach of Westminster Abbey.'

He adds that he can spare a full fortnight annually to run over and enjoy this collection.

We have sent him an address in Broad Sanctuary, and

another near Melton Mowbray, informing him at the same time that, if he possesses an arquebus, the breach is easily made; but we admit we feel less confidence than usual in our suggestions.

Another gentleman writes:—

'I have been boss of ———— (word indecipherable, but apparently beginning with T) for a short time, and am now prepared to invest 10,000,000 dollars in real estate in neighbourhood of fashionable noblemen's seats, and become typical squire.   What do you advise?'

Here it strikes us that elegant English rather than specific counsel best meets the case.

'We advise you,' we would reply, ' to follow the dictates of that star-spangled conscience which has conducted you so rapidly to affluence.   Should it prompt you to hail Columbia from our shores, we have no doubt that you will continue to get your money's worth.'

This, we flatter ourselves, leaves the gentleman's judgment practically unhampered.

In some cases we are completely foiled by want cf local knowledge.

Thus, we fear, we cannot assist our esteemed correspondent Alleghany Abe to discover an address in a place called Tenderloin. Indeed, we do not know of any city of that name.

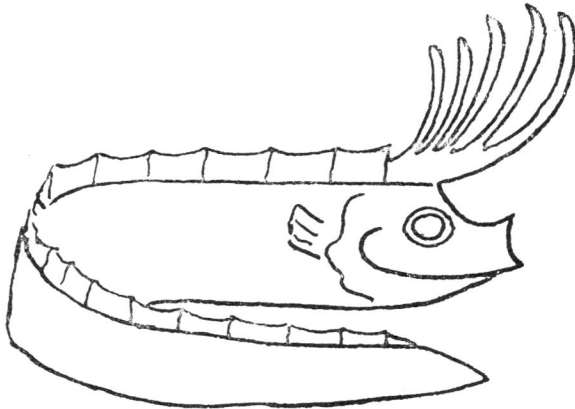

AUCTOR IPSE, OR TOMMYROTTER.
(TO BE FOUND GENERALLY IN DEEP WATER.)

Another question which baffles us concerns social precedence in Jeffersondavistown, County Belgravia; while the next makes us feel our architectural limitations acutely :—

'Whether is a Roccoco Rotunda in the style of the Renaissance, or a Castellated Wigwam modelled on the Parthenon, the most appropriate residence for a citizen of the greatest Nation on Earth?'

We can only recommend the citizen of the greatest Nation on Earth to settle it by spinning a quarter.

A fourth has given us some thought :—

'How many ancestors make what you call a gentleman in Europe? Here we need none, and I despise such distinctions; but, if necessary, could trace descent from Edward the Confessor.

'By the way, is Lady Grisetta Battlecock the second or third daughter of Lord Shuttledore, and is it true that she was engaged to Sir Hildebrand Hammersmith before her marriage?

'I am told they are distant relations of mine, hence my passing curiosity.'

After long deliberation we decided merely to despatch a copy of Debrett with the page turned down at Shuttledore, adorning our Republican correspondent's name on the packet with a hyphen and an Honourable.

Our tact has elicited recipes for three mixed drinks and an

invitation to the Pan-American Exhibition of 1910.

With this characteristic instance of the gratitude which Unsophisticated Opulence so generously lavishes upon Tactful Suggestion, we shall say farewell to our Readers. For one instant we raise the curtain of Reticence and, across the footlights of Literary Art, we bow in acknowledgment of the applause our honesty forbids us to disclaim. In the course of centuries the progress of civilization may render our treatise superfluous. Till then we would urge the Wealthy to leave at least one copy where it can always be found and instantly consulted.

Deportment for Dukes & Tips for Toffs

Deportment
for
DUKES
&Tips
for TOFFS

By BRUMMELL & BEAU

FIRST PUBLISHED IN 1900, this is the original deportment guide for the aristocracy. Among the areas of advice offered are: the dinner table, hunting, shooting, the ballroom, the precedence of personages, *conversation de société*, and the whole duty of the gentleman. An invaluable guide to manners and mores, this book is as indispensable to the modern aristocrat as it was over a hundred years ago.

'A telegram costs sixpence; there are
many acquaintances worth less than that.'

'A general conversation in the highest social strata may touch on politics,
partridges, and impropriety. The bourgeois may discuss clergymen and
internal complaints, and those in humble stations tripe and treason.'

'Avoid the vulgar and objectionable habit of conversing with
your fellow-travellers. Be on your guard when asked a civil
question; if you cannot answer rudely, do not reply at all.'

£7.99
ISBN 978 0 7123 5703 6